The Vital Nutrition cookbook

Recipes for energy and vitality

The Vital Nutrition cookbook

Recipes for energy and vitality

Jane McClenaghan

Published by: Vital Nutrition Ltd, PO Box 430, Belfast BT8 7YA www.vital-nutrition.co.uk
For more copies of this book, please email info@vital-nutrition.co.uk

Designed by: Jill Morrison, Cheah Design
Food stylists: Jean McClenaghan & Jill Morrison
Recipe photographs: Sue Spencer
Food, location and cover photographs: Stephen Nicholas Wilson

Publisher's Note: The information in this book is intended as a general guide and not as a
substitute for professional medical advice and treatment. Always consult your health practitioner
before starting a nutrition programme if you have any health concerns.

ISBN 978-0-9927187-0-1

Printed in the UK by W & G Baird

contents

Acknowledgements

This book is the culmination of over five years' work and it would never have seen the light of day without the help of some great people.

First of all, my brilliant parents for encouraging and supporting me all the way, and being there for me, no matter what.

Thanks to Nev, chief taster, for his astonishingly hard-working taste buds and enthusiastic 'yums'. Kelly, Sara, Amanda, Steph, Jo, Jean and Sarah, thank you for your red pens and proofreading skills.

Sue Spencer and Steve 'Wizzy' Wilson, your stunning photographs make the book look mouth-wateringly delicious. Jill, what can I say? You have done an amazing job.

Nikki Jarvis, you gave me the nudge in the direction of self-publishing that I needed to make this book happen. Thank you to Framar Health, Broighter Gold and Jackson Greens – just some of my local, independent suppliers who provided ingredients and photo opportunities galore!

Bethan, Owen and Sam – keep stirring, whizzing, licking, tasting and cooking. You are the next generation of foodies.

To all of my family, friends and clients who munched, crunched, chewed and sampled the recipes, thanks for your honest feedback.

A great big, heartfelt thanks to the lot of you!

I love food ..

…and am passionate about the powerful effects that eating good quality, fresh, local food has on our mind, body and soul. I want to inject a little positivity and fun back into your kitchen to help vitalise your energy levels and ignite your zest for life.

I don't believe in fad diets, crazy quick fixes or extreme nutritional makeovers and you don't need to do a total cupboard clearout to eat well. Instead, make some small changes to your eating habits and you'll soon get that spring back in your step. In *The Vital Nutrition Cookbook* you'll find ideas galore for transforming the way you think about healthy eating, and yes, there is a place for chocolate!

At the start of the book you will find a bit of nutritional advice and some shopping ideas to inspire you to make a change or two to your diet. The second half of the book is jam-packed with simple, low GL recipes that I hope you will enjoy cooking and eating as much as I do. Feel free to add a dash of this and a splash of the other to put your own stamp on the recipes. These are just my ideas to get you started and inspire you to cook from fresh every day of the week.

I've created and developed these recipes over time. They are designed to be quick and easy so that you can rustle up something nutritious at any time of the day. The photographs tell it as it is – no sprays, cotton wool or fancy tampering were used to enhance the look of the food in any of the pics; just good quality, tasty produce in all its glory. Happy cooking!

Jumpstart
your energy levels!

It's time to get real

If you want to feel energised, you'll need to eat real food – fruit, vegetables, wholegrains, good quality fish and meat. Fast food, sweets, crisps, chocolate, takeaways and ready meals may be appealing if you can't be bothered cooking, but they will sap your energy, trigger sugar cravings and leave you hungry for more.

Nutritious food does not have to be boring or bland. Long gone are the days when the idea of healthy eating was some brown rice and a few sad looking lentils (eaten from a wooden bowl whilst wearing sandals!). Eating good food is one of life's greatest pleasures, so enjoy it. Liven up meals with seasonings, sauces and spices and vary your diet so you don't get bored.

There are plenty of shortcuts to make delicious, healthy food in a flash. Venture into your local supermarket and check out the frozen food aisle. You'll find good quality frozen fish (beside the fish fingers), vegetables (beside the frozen pizza) and fruit (beside the ice cream). Or have a look in the 'World Foods' section to bag some healthy sauces (e.g. harissa or curry pastes), ready-cooked brown rice or buckwheat noodles.

The most important rule of all = 80:20

You will not find any finger-wagging or extreme ideas in this book. Balance is the key. As long as you eat well 80% of the time, a little bit of what you fancy does no harm at all if balanced with a healthy, nutritious diet. Go out and share a meal with friends, have a chocolate bar every now and again, or enjoy fish and chips at the seaside. Just remember to sit down, savour the moment and realise that these foods are treats, not core elements of your diet.

Jumpstart your energy levels

Most of us are living on a blood sugar rollercoaster without realising it, swinging through highs and lows as we bombard our body with stimulants and junk food, skipping meals and thriving on high stress levels. Is it any wonder we end up feeling tired, grumpy and craving sweet stuff?

If you are serious about jumpstarting your energy levels, you'll need to have a little bit of know-how on keeping your blood sugar in perfect balance.

There are five golden rules for blood sugar balance:

1. **Break your fast**
2. **Get grazing**
3. **Power yourself with protein**
4. **Quit the energy zappers**
5. **Get down with the GL**

Read on to find out more…

1. Break your fast

How do you feel about the first meal of the day? Are you a breakfast eater or a breakfast hater?

Which of these statements reflects your attitude to breakfast?

a. Even the thought of breakfast makes me feel nauseous – there is no way I'm doing that!

b. I haven't got time to eat breakfast – mornings in my house are hectic enough without having to feed myself too!

c. Breakfast is my favourite meal of the day – I can't leave the house without it.

If you answered a.

Blood sugar levels are low when we wake up as we haven't eaten since the night before. If you wake up feeling queasy or with a bit of a headache, chances are you are riding the blood sugar rollercoaster.

If it works better for you, think of breakfast as a snack rather than a meal. Eat a little something first thing, then have your proper breakfast mid-morning. Even something small is better than nothing at all. Half a slice of toast with sugar-free peanut butter, a piece of fruit with some nuts, or even just a spoonful of yoghurt will help you break the fast and fuel your body first thing. Breakfast doesn't have to be a big meal, but you do need to eat something within 45 minutes of getting up if you want to get your blood sugar levels balanced and start your day feeling energised.

If you answered b.

Is that because you tend to hit the snooze button a few times before you crawl out of bed?

Once your energy levels start to improve you will be sleeping better, so you will wake up feeling refreshed and energised before the alarm clock screeches in your ear. Although this might seem like a far-fetched idea at the minute, it is true. I've seen the evidence with plenty of clients in my nutritional practice over the years.

If you are not a morning person, plan what you are going to eat the night before, even if this just means making sure the table is set for breakfast.

Don't put too many demands on yourself first thing – just sit at a table and eat something light. Try a quick bowl of porridge that you have made in the microwave, or a yoghurt and berry smoothie that you whizzed up the night before and stored in the fridge (you could even drink this while getting the kids ready for school, or as you are putting on your socks!).

If you answered c.

Great stuff! You are already one step ahead of the game. Keep a note of what you eat for breakfast over the next week or so. Use the food diary on page 175 to keep a check on your grub and help keep your blood sugar levels in perfect balance! Think outside the cereal box – have a look at the breakfast chapter (starting on page 48) for loads of nutritious and delicious breakfast ideas to add variety to your diet.

Why is breakfast so important?

So what's the big deal anyway? Why is breakfast so important? Well, if you eat breakfast you are providing your body with energy, nutrients and fuel so you can function at your best. If you skip breakfast, your body has to create energy from somewhere else, usually your adrenal glands.

Your adrenal glands are located on top of your kidneys and produce stress hormones, including adrenalin and cortisol. If you go without breakfast, your body will trigger a surge of adrenalin into your bloodstream to give you a quick hit of energy (and stress) to get you going.

Hang on a minute – all you are doing is getting the bus to work/driving the kids to school/doing the ironing. Do you really need an adrenalin rush first thing in the morning for that? This unnecessary adrenalin kick is probably making you stressed, irritable and a bit grumpy. Wouldn't it be easier just to have a small snack rather than feel like this every day?

What time is your breakfast?

Do you eat first thing, fairly soon after you get up, or do you leave breakfast until later – maybe when you get into work or at your 10 o'clock tea break?

Breakfast at 10am is fine as long as you get up at 9.30am! Don't forget, if you wake at 7am and your breakfast is not until mid morning then you've been running on empty and your body has been triggering the release of adrenal hormones unnecessarily.

Make sure you eat something within 30 to 45 minutes of getting up. This means you are fuelling your body with food, rather than adrenalin. Remember, even a small snack is better than nothing at all.

If you really can't face breakfast, why not drink something, rather than eat? Most health food shops sell good quality, natural protein powders made from ingredients like hemp, chia or quinoa. Just blend with a bit of milk, put into a flask and drink on your way to work. Have a look at the smoothie recipes on page 50 for an easy, portable breakfast.

2. Get grazing

Eating little and often is key to keeping your body fuelled and sustaining your energy levels. In the olden days of nutritional advice, we were told not to snack between meals and eat nothing after 6pm – unfortunately that left us with cravings, bad moods and low energy levels. Most nutrition experts now agree that it is better to fuel your body little and often – five smaller meals a day rather than the traditional three square meals.

As a general rule of thumb, aim to eat every three to four hours. This usually translates as three meals and two or three small snacks a day, which tends to fit in with most people's daily schedule. So your day might go a little something like this:

7am:	eat breakfast
10am:	tea break at work – eat a small snack
1pm:	lunch break
4pm:	tea break time again
7pm:	dinner

If you have kids to feed and want your family to eat their dinner together, you might have a slightly different routine. Perhaps you eat your evening meal a bit earlier to fit in with the children's bedtime and then your day might look more like this:

8am:	breakfast
12pm:	an early lunch
3pm:	snack
5pm:	dinner
8pm:	suppertime snack

You will soon work out what fits best with your schedule. If you are not used to snacking between meals, it's a good idea to reduce your portion sizes at mealtimes. Portion sizes should roughly be:

Breakfast:	about the size of two cupped hands
Snacks:	about the size of one cupped hand
Lunch:	enough to cover the surface area of two flat palms
Dinner:	about the same size as lunch

3. Power yourself with protein

Think protein! Having a little portion of protein with each meal and snack will help to keep your energy levels sustained and your appetite under control. You'll soon notice that you don't get so many cravings for sugary snacks and junk food, as protein helps to keep you full for longer.

When we think of protein, most of us tend to think eggs, meat and fish, but there are plenty of other choices too. You'll find protein in your diet in:

- Eggs – you can eat an egg a day if you like. They're a great source of protein and contrary to what we once believed will not increase cholesterol levels.

- Meat – always choose good quality, lean meat. Visit your butcher or farmers' market to buy local and organic if possible.

- Fish – choose sustainable options such as pollock or mackerel.

- Chicken – free range or organic is the best choice and readily available in most butchers, supermarkets and farm shops.

- Nuts – make a great snack food. Just remember we are not talking about the salted or dry-roasted varieties! Choose from almonds, hazelnuts, cashews, pecans, macadamia, walnuts or brazils.

- Seeds – not just for the birds! Seeds are packed full of essential nutrients and are a great protein source. Try sesame, sunflower, pumpkin, flax (sometimes known as linseed), chia, hemp. They taste great lightly toasted in a dry frying pan and sprinkled over salads. Flavoured varieties are available such as herby, spicy or chilli.

- Pulses – peas, beans and lentils are a cost-effective and healthy source of protein.

- Dairy products – the best choices are low-fat natural yoghurt and cottage cheese as they are higher in protein.

- Tofu – choose firm tofu for a vegetarian alternative in stir-fries or curries.

- Quinoa – a South American seed that is easy to cook and can be used as an alternative to rice.

- Houmous – check the ingredient list and only put it in your shopping basket if you recognise all the ingredients. The full fat version tends to be healthier. Traditionally the ingredients in houmous are chickpeas, olive oil, tahini (sesame seed paste), lemon juice, garlic, salt & pepper – all good stuff. You'll find flavoured houmous in your local supermarket or deli; try a few to see which you prefer.

- Tahini – this is sesame seed paste, an ingredient in houmous.

- Nut butters – there's a great choice of nut butters available now. You can get sugar-free peanut butter and delicious almond, hazel, cashew or brazil nut butters, which make a good snack with a couple of oatcakes – a great alternative to a sugary biscuit with your cuppa. Check out your local health food shop for some tasty varieties.

4. Quit the energy zappers

Sugar and caffeine are the biggest energy zappers in our diet and yet they are exactly what we go for when we need a quick pick-me-up or afternoon energy boost. Yes, they do give us a quick hit of energy, but almost as soon as we have eaten that chocolate bar, guzzled that can of cola or slurped that quick coffee, we need more to keep the high.

Beware hidden sugars! Maybe you gave up sugar in your tea years ago, you only have chocolate as an occasional treat and you wouldn't touch candy floss with a barge pole. So far so good, but what about the low-fat cereal you have for breakfast, the four or five portions of fruit you eat to reach your healthy five-a-day target, the low-cal biscuit you snack on mid-morning and the light yoghurt you have every day with lunch?

If you have tended towards a low-fat diet until now, you may be consuming more sugar than you realise. Years of low-fat dieting has meant we now eat more sugar than ever as most processed, low-fat foods tend to be high in sugar (to make them taste of something). We've become a nation of yo-yo dieters, riding the blood sugar rollercoaster, feeling exhausted and fed up.

If you are a fruit lover, you could be doing yourself more harm than good if you munch your way through dried fruit, grapes, tropical fruit and fruit juices to keep yourself nutritionally topped up. Fruit can be a major source of sugar in our diet. Fruit sugar (known as fructose) has the same energy sapping impact as a chocolate bar or fizzy drink.

Of course fruit is not bad, per se. It's just that we tend to eat a little too much of it and favour it over vegetables. As long as you stick to two or three portions a day, choose lower sugar fruit and favour vegetables instead, then the fruit sugar thing won't be an issue.

Get rid of low-fat foods – they are not doing your energy levels or your waistline any favours.

Instead, eat *more* of these nutritious and delicious foods:

- more vegetables
- more wholegrains
- more unprocessed foods
- more nuts
- more seeds
- more oily fish

Look out for these energy enemies:

- avoid foods with more than 15g sugar per 100g as these are classed as high sugar
- avoid artificial sweeteners (common in low-fat yoghurts in particular) – they'll just make you crave more sugary stuff
- avoid low-fat foods as they tend to be laden with sugar

Are you eating too much hidden sugar?

Do you prefer tropical fruit, grapes and bananas?	Opt for lower sugar fruit such as apples, pears, plums, berries, cherries, kiwi and citrus fruit. Generally any fruit that grows in a temperate climate like the UK has a lower sugar level than fruit grown in tropical climates.
Do you snack on dried fruit?	Munch on fresh fruit instead – but no more than 2 or 3 portions a day and always the lower sugar options.
Do you drink fruit juice?	Dilute juices half and half with water to reduce the sugar hit.
Do you eat more than 3 pieces of fruit a day?	Reduce to 2 or 3 portions of low sugar fruit. As an alternative, try snacking on raw vegetables like carrot sticks, sugar snap peas or celery with houmous.
Do you buy low-fat foods?	Check the sugar content – if it is higher than 15g per 100g, put it back on the shelf.
Do you fill more than half your plate with carbohydrates like potatoes, rice or pasta?	About a fistful of low GL carbohydrates (see page 28), makes an ideal portion size for main meals.

Day	How many cups?	How do you feel?
Monday		
Tuesday		
Wednesday		
Thursday		
Friday		
Saturday		
Sunday		

So what of the odd cup of coffee?

Caffeine triggers your adrenal glands to produce adrenalin, which is why we feel energised almost as soon as we drink our morning cuppa. For proof of this, imagine how you would feel if you went a bit overboard on your caffeine intake and had one cup too many – maybe a bit jittery, you might notice your heart is pounding, or the palms of your hands are sweaty. Now imagine how you feel when you are stressed or anxious... Jittery? Pounding heart? Sweaty palms? Not so much of a coincidence, as both stress and caffeine trigger a surge of adrenalin into your bloodstream, triggering the fight-or-flight reaction.

When the adrenalin wears off it leaves you feeling a bit flat, fatigued or fed up – nothing another cuppa won't cure, eh? If you want to get off the blood sugar rollercoaster then you'll need to seriously cut the caffeine.

It's a good idea to keep a caffeine diary for a week to work out how many caffeinated drinks you have a day. Use the table on page 24 to keep a tally of how much you are drinking and how it makes you feel. Once you have done this you can start to reduce your intake – just do it slowly so you don't end up with headaches and withdrawal symptoms.

How much is too much?

The more caffeine we drink, the higher our tolerance for it. For some people three cups of coffee would leave them feeling wired, but for others this is just enough for them to feel 'normal'.

The Food Standards Agency suggests that the average healthy adult can safely consume 300mg of caffeine a day – that's about three or four cups of tea or a couple of coffees a day. For pregnant women, the advice is a maximum of 200mg of caffeine a day: one strong coffee or a couple of teas.

But … here's the rub. A recent study by the University of Glasgow analysed coffees from twenty different coffee shops and discovered that the caffeine content varied from 51mg to 322mg per cup! It seems that the massive difference in caffeine content is due to the type of bean used and the roasting and grinding methods, but the most significant difference was the amount of coffee put into the espresso maker by the barista.

Although caffeine gets negative press, it's not all bad news. Some studies show that coffee may reduce our cancer risk as it is packed full of phenolic substances with antioxidant properties. Other studies have suggested that coffee drinkers may have a lower risk of cardiovascular disease, tooth decay, gout, type 2 diabetes and Alzheimers.

As a rough guide, I would suggest no more than a couple of coffees a day. Rather than gulping your way through six or eight cups of instant coffee, treat yourself to one or two cups of really good coffee (just don't make it too strong!).

If you are a tea drinker, about three or four cups of tea a day should be about right, depending on whether you like your tea weak or prefer a good strong cup of 'builder's tea'. Obviously if you already drink less than this, then don't increase your intake.

Herbal teas have had a bit of a re-invention over the last few years. Most supermarkets and health food shops stock a good variety, so you should be able to find one or two that you like. Check out chai tea with cinnamon and ginger or green tea for blood sugar balance. If the sugar monster strikes try licorice tea. It has a lovely natural sweetness and licorice has been shown to help support blood sugar balance.

We all know that fizzy drinks are packed full of sugar, but if you go for the diet versions thinking they are a healthy option, then think again. Basically you are treating yourself to a can of chemicals. Diet drinks are loaded with artificial sweeteners like aspartame which have been found to trigger sugar cravings and have been associated with a wide range of health problems, including obesity.

Try replacing fizzy drinks with apple juice diluted half and half with sparkling water for a drink that is fairly low in sugar, tastes sweet and will give you the fizzy sensation you crave.

5. Get down with the GL

Once upon a time carbohydrates were categorised as simple or complex. Then along came the GI, or glycaemic index, which tells us how efficient a food is at keeping our energy levels sustained.

Carbohydrate gets broken down into glucose in the body, which is used by our cells for energy. The GI is a score, rated between 1 and 100, to measure this and tell us how fast or slow this breakdown happens. So the higher the GI, the bigger the glucose (sugar) hit. High GI foods like chocolate or dried fruit give us an instant sugar rush, whereas foods with a low or medium GI (pulses and porridge) provide us with a more sustained supply of energy.

Straightforward and easy to understand, right? Stay with me for this one, there's a wee bit more to it. The GI measures the effects of 100g of a food on your blood sugar levels, but how often do we eat exactly 100g of any food? We usually measure our grub in portion sizes, don't we?

Some foods like porridge, brown rice and watermelon are given a high GI score which is a little confusing, until you understand that the GI does not take portion sizes into account.

With advances in research and the development of scientific ideas, nutritional science changes all the time. So the new kid on the block is the glycaemic load (affectionately known as the GL). This little number does take portion size into account, giving a more accurate estimation of the effect food will have on your blood sugar levels.

Let's take watermelon as an example. It scores a whopping 72 for GI (remember the highest score is 100). When it's broken down to portion sizes, a great big slice of juicy watermelon has a tiny little GL score of 3.6 (anything over 20 is considered high). See how confusing this could be if you allowed scores, tables and charts to help you decide what to eat?

Let's keep it simple. Here it is in a nutshell:

Low GL foods	High GL foods
• high fibre	• lacking fibre
• low sugar	• high sugar
• unprocessed	• white, refined
• sustained energy release	• quick hit

Easy ways to choose low GL

If you usually eat this:	Swap it for this:
White bread	Wholegrain, stoneground, sourdough or rye bread
White rice	Brown basmati rice or quinoa
White pasta	Wholegrain or spelt pasta cooked *al dente* to keep it lower GL
Low-fat biscuits	Higher fibre, lower sugar, oat based biscuits
Mashed potatoes	Baby boiled new potatoes, sweet potatoes or potato salad, as cold potatoes have a lower GL
Refined or sugary cereals	Porridge or low sugar granola
Biscuits	An oatcake with sugar-free peanut butter
Chocolate bar	A few squares of dark chocolate with a small handful of brazil nuts
Dried fruit	Fresh fruit
Low-fat flavoured yoghurt	Natural or Greek yoghurt with fresh fruit

What's in
your basket?

How do you shop?

Do you rush around the supermarket frantically trying to decide what to have for tea, or do you sit down and plan your weekly menu, make a shopping list and only buy what you set out to?

Good food does not have to break the bank, blow the budget and leave you out of pocket. There are plenty of economical ways to eat healthily, even when money is tight.

With just a little imagination and a few carefully selected ingredients, your store cupboard can contain all the basics for a range of nutritious and delicious meals.

Supermarket deals, such as '3 for 2' offers, or 'buy one get one free', are often for foods and drinks that are not going to do your health any favours. Here are a few ideas to help you become a savvy shopper and make the most of your food budget.

1. Buy local

Every community has its local food heroes: people who are passionate about growing good quality, healthy food in (and for) their local neighbourhood. Here in Northern Ireland, farming has been the lifeblood of our community for generations and we have a wealth of artisan producers. Maybe you'll find a few hidden gems you didn't realise were on your doorstep: low GI bread from your local baker, fresh broccoli grown in a field less than a mile away or some locally reared beef that has enjoyed the great outdoors on a farm around the corner.

Instead of relying on big supermarkets to provide your food, why not check out your local farmers' market, greengrocer, butcher and deli to discover what's hot in your neighbourhood? Sometimes the best bargains can be found in these smaller, local shops and you could even be lucky enough to meet the person who grew your vegetables, baked your bread or fed your chicken.

Discover who grows, rears, bakes, makes and cooks in your community and celebrate local food.

It's also worth asking around to see if there is a food cooperative or box scheme in your area. You are likely to get really good quality ingredients at a fraction of the price you would pay elsewhere, as these set-ups can buy foods in bulk at close to cost price. Follow them on Facebook and Twitter to get an idea of the type of food they supply and when and where they deliver.

2. Shop around

If you do most of your shopping in one of the bigger supermarkets, you'll notice that they often compare prices with each other in a bid to win your hard-earned cash.

If you can be flexible about when you do your shopping, go towards the end of the day as that's when lots of foods with a short use-by date are marked down in price. Be careful not to buy bags of fresh food that you won't use though, as it's more than likely to end up in the bin, costing you money rather than saving it.

It's a good idea to buy non-perishable items in bulk. If you spot an offer on tinned foods like pulses, tomatoes or fish, take advantage of the deal and buy a few.

Check out your local Asian supermarket to source some of the key ingredients of a healthy diet at a fraction of the cost. Herbs and spices, tinned pulses and coconut milk as well as healthy fats and oils, such as olive oil and coconut oil, can be found in these shops at a greatly reduced price.

3. Shop regularly

Shop two or three times a week for perishable items like fruit and vegetables. This way you will have less food waste and just use what you buy, rather than throwing lots of food away. Have a chat to your greengrocer and see what day they get their deliveries so that you know you are getting really fresh produce.

It is estimated that the average UK household throws away a third of the food it purchases.

Just think what you could do if your food bill was cut by one third every week!

4. Buy frozen foods

If frozen food brings to mind images of soggy carrots and fish fingers, think again! A quick look around this section in the supermarket will provide you with a selection of nutritious ingredients for eating well on a budget. Frozen berries are a fraction of the price of the fresh versions; you'll find a range of vegetables for steaming, stir-frying or roasting to add variety to your meals, and frozen fish makes an ideal standby for an economical curry or quick dinner.

Having your freezer well stocked means there is always something healthy that you can throw together at dinnertime.

In the frozen food section look out for:

- Herbs & spices – basil, parsley, garlic, ginger and chilli are readily available and make a fantastic alternative to fresh herbs and spices, as they will last for ages. They can work out a little more expensive than the fresh stuff, but can be much more convenient and have less chance of ending up in the bin, especially if you live on your own or don't use these ingredients much.

- Fish – frozen-at-sea fish are frozen within four hours of being caught, so freshness is guaranteed. Just remember to look out for the MSC logo to make sure your fish is from a sustainable source. Keep an eye out for alternatives to the usual cod and haddock – coley and pollock might be more sustainable options.

- Vegetables – it's not just peas and sweetcorn that you'll find in the frozen vegetable section these days. Slightly more exotic choices such as char-grilled Mediterranean vegetables or Oriental stir-fry veg are just some of the newcomers to this section. Frozen peppers are great and you can add them to just about anything.

- Fruit – berries freeze really well, so it's worth keeping an eye out for these when they are not in season, as they tend to be a little cheaper than fresh berries at certain times of the year. Frozen

berries make a great standby for an impressive looking dessert if you are caught on the hop by visitors. Check out my Berry Nice Compote recipe on page 154 for a delicious dessert that will impress any guest.

- Ice cream – no, this is not a misprint! A little bit of ice cream is fine to include in your diet, as long as it is an occasional treat, and you choose really good quality ice cream. Go for the slightly more expensive versions, with real ingredients. Cream, milk, eggs, sugar and vanilla are what you should find in your ice cream – not vegetable fat, colourings, emulsifiers, stabilisers and gums.

5. Make in bulk

Throw in a few extra ingredients to make a little more than you are going to eat and freeze the leftovers in portion sizes for a healthy lunch or dinner on another day.

If you are cooking up quinoa or dried legumes (beans and lentils), why not cook the whole bag and freeze in individual sized freezer bags, so you always have a quick protein source handy for soups, stews, lunches or curries.

6. Make the most of your ingredients

The most expensive ingredient on our plate tends to be meat. Using meat as a condiment, rather than the main event of your meals could mean dramatically cutting the cost of your food bill. Bulk out bolognese or casseroles with a cupful of lentils or eke out a curry with the addition of a tin of chickpeas.

Peas, beans and lentils are a valuable source of fibre and protein, helping to keep you full for longer, but they are also very cheap ingredients. I would suggest using dried lentils (Puy, green, red or yellow) as these don't have to be soaked before cooking. Dried beans, on the other hand, do need soaking, so for convenience, buy them tinned. Again, check out your local Asian supermarket for good value pulses. They may not be the brands you are used to, but as long as they are tinned in water only (without salt or sugar added), they are a cheap and healthy addition to your diet.

7. Store cupboard essentials

Stock your store cupboard with key ingredients that you can rely on to make a healthy meal, such as:

- Oats

  Oats are perfect for an economical and healthy breakfast. Either make into porridge, or use as the base for homemade granolas and mueslis (try my Muesli with a Twist on page 56, or Orange and Vanilla Granola on page 58). Granola and muesli tend to be expensive if you are buying them, but cheap as chips and easy to throw together if you make them yourself.

- Eggs

  Eggs are the perfect standby food: extremely versatile, high in protein and gentle on the wallet. They make an ideal meal at any time of the day and we can eat an egg a day without any negative health consequences. Go to work on an egg with boiled, poached or scrambled for breakfast, in a salad or wholemeal pitta for lunch or as a frittata or omelette for dinner.

- Tinned pulses

  Just by adding a tin of pulses to curry, soup, chilli or stir-fry, you'll get an additional portion or two for pennies, which can feed another member of the family or be frozen for a quick dinner at another time.

- Herbs and spices

  A few herbs and spices in your spice rack will make all the difference to mealtimes. The ones I use a lot are smoked paprika, cumin, mixed spice, black pepper, cardamom pods, chilli powder, cinnamon, turmeric and garam masala, and these are used in lots of my recipes. Combined with some fresh garlic, root ginger, a dash of low salt soy sauce and a chilli or two, you'll have a spice selection that can liven up any meal.

- Tinned fish

  Tinned mackerel and sardines can contribute to your target of eating oily fish two to three times a week. They can be added to a

lunchbox with some salad and a few oatcakes to sustain your energy levels throughout the afternoon or as an ingredient for fishcakes for a tasty dinner.

- Tinned tomatoes or passata

  The base for a great curry, chilli or casserole, not only are tinned tomatoes and passata cheap ingredients, but they are also highly nutritious and will count as one of your five a day.

- Coconut milk

  Swap ready-made curry sauces and takeaways for a quick and simple homemade version. Add a dash of lime juice and a dollop of Thai curry paste to a tin of coconut milk, throw in some fish, chicken or prawns and a handful or two of fresh or frozen vegetables and you have yourself some of the best fast food you'll taste.

- Coconut oil

  Coconut oil is the perfect oil for cooking, as it can withstand higher temperatures than more delicate oils like olive, sunflower or vegetable oil. Solid at room temperature, coconut oil can be used as a healthier alternative to margarines as a spread, or in recipes for cooking, roasting and baking. Emerging evidence shows that coconut oil is a healthy addition to our modern diet. Although it contains saturated fat, these are medium chain fatty acids (MUFAs), which have been associated with protection against obesity and weight gain and seem to have a balancing effect on cholesterol.

8. Pack a lunch

It makes sense to take a lunch to work with you. That way you are sure to eat a nourishing mid-day meal and you'll probably save yourself some cash into the bargain. Your lunch portion should be enough to cover the surface area of the palms of both hands and include some protein, slow release carbohydrate and some form of vegetable (maybe as a soup, salad or crudités).

Try some of these ideas for a healthy lunchbox:

- Homemade soups – include beans or lentils for your protein hit and make a big pot so you can freeze it in portion sizes for another day. If you use low salt stock cubes you will also be eating less salt than tinned soup. I have loads of tasty soup recipes for you in the lunch section starting on page 72.

- Filled wholemeal pitta pockets – Buy a pack and have different fillings each day of the week for a tasty lunch. Fill with tinned fish, houmous, cottage cheese or chicken for protein and bulk out with grated carrot, celery, salad leaves, tomatoes and peppers for your veg portion.

- Leftovers – invest in a food flask and pack it with the remains of last night's dinner or fill with soup for a warming lunch.

- A few oatcakes, some chopped raw vegetables (think carrot sticks, celery, peppers, sugar snap peas) with some houmous or cheese make a tasty alternative to a sandwich at lunchtime.

- Take your own water bottle to work instead of sugary fizzy drinks or expensive bottled water. If you usually spend a couple of quid on your morning cuppa from the local barista, why not invest in a mini cafetière and make a posh coffee at work. As long as you are not guzzling gallons of the stuff, and limiting your coffee intake to one or two good cups every day, it won't deplete your energy levels too much. Even better, if you want to make a really positive lifestyle change why not swap your morning cappuccino for a cup of green or herbal tea instead?

- Pack a couple of pieces of fruit, some natural yoghurt and some vegetable sticks with mini pots of houmous so that you have some tasty treats to snack on too.

9. Eat more fish

Make the right choice with the fish you eat and you'll save a fortune. Ignore the expensive cod, monkfish and salmon and instead opt for the lesser-eaten (and generally more sustainable) fish like dab or bream, mackerel or sardines. These are widely available and if you have a fish counter in your supermarket or a local fishmonger, it is worth asking for ideas on cooking. That way you'll learn a bit more about the fish you are eating and widen your repertoire of weekly recipes.

We all know that fish is good for us and that we should probably be eating more of it, but how do you know it is sustainable? One way to find out is by asking your fishmonger. Where did the fish come from? Is it line caught? Is it approved by 'MSC'? – this is the Marine Stewardship Council and is the gold standard accreditation for sustainable fish stocks in the UK. Look out for the distinctive blue logo to be sure.

You can find out more on The Marine Stewardship's website www.goodfishguide.co.uk or download the 'Good Fish Guide' app for up to date info on what fish to eat at different times of the year.

10. Plan ahead

Plan your meals and make a list. Most families have a few firm favourites on their weekly menu. Spag bol or chicken curry spring to mind. Have a look through the recipe pages, choose a few dishes that you like the look of and plan what you are going to eat over the next week or so to help you make a list of what ingredients you will need before you make a trip to the shops. This will help you make healthier choices, and will ensure you just buy what you need, rather than what looks tempting at the time.

You will notice that a lot of the recipes use similar ingredients, or you can adapt the recipes according to what you have in your fridge, cupboard or larder, so you won't waste anything.

Check what's in your cupboards and plan ideas around this. For example, if you have three tins of tomatoes and a jar of curry paste, then you've got a good idea that at least one of your meals for the week will be a quick curry.

Planning ahead also means you are less likely to throw food out – use up what you've got before buying new stuff. If you have some fruit that is getting past its best, use it to make a smoothie or poach in spices and low GL agave syrup for a healthy dessert. Check out the recipe for Lightly Spiced Poached Pears on page 146.

11. Make the most of fresh herbs

Herbs can transform a mediocre meal into a delicious dinner. Dried herbs are fine to use, but the taste doesn't compare to the fresh stuff.

Fresh herbs are far too expensive to add to the compost bin, so blitz any combination of leftover herbs with a bit of olive or rapeseed oil and some lemon juice. Season with salt and pepper to make a herby pesto that you can add to almost any dish. You can freeze this herby oil mixture in ice cube trays for a pop of flavour when you need it. Check out the Salsa Verde recipe on page 130.

If you fancy growing your own, it's simple to do and you'll be rewarded with a constant supply of fresh herbs. All you need are a couple of small pots, a packet of seeds and a sunny windowsill, or a small patch in your garden. Just remember to water the seeds every now and again and then sit back and watch them grow!

Grow what you use and use what you grow. Think about which herbs you use most in your cooking – parsley, basil and coriander tend to be the most popular in the supermarkets, but maybe you prefer sage, rosemary or thyme.

Some Mediterranean herbs like basil don't fare too well outside in our cooler climate, so you may have more success growing them during the summer months in a greenhouse or on a sunny windowsill. Some of the more hardy herbs like thyme, rosemary and parsley are perfectly suited to our climate.

12. Take some healthy shortcuts!

On days when you feel zapped by the time you get in from work, the last thing you will want to do is spend ages cooking dinner. Most of the recipes in this book are quick and easy to prepare. If you have one or two recipes that you can turn to when you need a healthy, fast meal, you can't go too far wrong.

How about these quick meal ideas?

- Stir-fry, using frozen vegetables and prawns with a dash of soy sauce, some garlic, a little ginger and a wee bit of chilli.

- Have some packets of pre-cooked, steamed brown rice handy. Just throw into a wok, add some protein (a handful of pulses, some ready-cooked chicken or a little leftover beef), a few extra vegetables (maybe some peas, spinach, celery and chopped peppers) and you have a meal. Fast and simple.

- Tinned fish or eggs can form the basis of a good meal even when the cupboards are bare. Serve on some low GL style bread with a quickly thrown together side salad of tomatoes and green leaves and you have a decent, filling supper.

- Although we tend to think of soup as a lunchtime meal, it can make a nourishing and fast dinner. Just remember to include some form of protein so that you are not hungry soon after. Have a look at pages 20-21 for good protein sources.

- A quick chicken salad makes a perfect healthy dinner. Grate some carrot, slice a couple of tomatoes, add a handful of salad leaves, some of those fresh herbs you've been growing, toasted seeds and dress with one of the salad dressings on page 104 for a healthy mid-week tea.

Damaged and dangerous oil!

If you are using sunflower or vegetable oil in your pan, then stop right there! When these delicate polyunsaturated oils are heated to a high temperature they become damaged, which is bad news for our health. For a healthier alternative choose these oils for cooking:

- Coconut oil (my favourite oil for cooking)
- Clarified butter (ghee)
- Avocado oil
- Rapeseed oil

Cold-pressed olive oil can support long-term blood sugar balance, so don't skip on salad dressings.

Your shopping list

If you are planning to change a few things in your diet, make a list of some new foods that you want to buy.

Check out the recipe pages, see what takes your fancy and plan your weekly menu around that. There is a 7 day plan on pages 172-173, with ideas and suggestions to get you started.

Here are a few key essentials for your shopping list:

- Fresh fruit and vegetables.

- Some sustainable fish. This can be fresh, frozen or tinned, just remember to get enough so that you can include it two or three times a week in your diet.

- Nuts and seeds. Maybe some milled flaxseed to sprinkle over your breakfast, almonds, hazelnuts and walnuts for a quick snack or some pumpkin and sunflower seeds to add a tasty crunch to salads.

- Natural or Greek-style yoghurt for snacks or dessert.

- Butter, coconut oil, rapeseed oil or olive oil for spreading, cooking and drizzling.

- Herbs and spices, in particular cinnamon and turmeric, as these have been associated with blood sugar balance and immune support.

- A big bar of organic, dark chocolate (at least 70% cocoa solids). For health reasons only, of course!

GOOd morning sunshine!

Breakfast recipes

Smoothies

I'd suggest going freestyle with your smoothies, using up whatever fruit you have and throwing in a bit of avocado or yoghurt to make yourself a quick and tasty energy-boosting breakfast.

Green one

Big handful of watercress

1 nectarine (or peach, or pear)

¼ avocado

A handful of fresh mint leaves

¼ cup apple juice or coconut water

1 cup water

Pink one

2 big handfuls of mixed berries
(fresh or frozen)

250g natural yoghurt
(or coconut milk)

Optional extra –
agave syrup to sweeten

White one

1 ripe avocado

1 nectarine or peach

1 small banana (not too ripe)

2 dsp natural yoghurt

½ cup almond milk

Method

Place the ingredients into your blender and blitz to the desired consistency.

Vital Tip:

Don't go overboard with the fruit content, and add in a wee bit of protein, like some yoghurt or milled seeds, to keep your smoothies low GL.

Perfect Porridge

Porridge has stood the test of time as a popular breakfast for generations, providing a source of slow release carbohydrate to help to keep energy levels maintained throughout the day. Try these ideas for porridge with a tasty twist.

Berry & Cinnamon Porridge

A handful of porridge oats per person

A shake of ground cinnamon

A handful of berries (fresh or frozen)

1-2 dsp milled seeds per person

Spiced Porridge

A handful of porridge oats per person

½ tsp cinnamon

½ tsp nutmeg

¼ tsp ground ginger

A handful of walnuts or pecans

Agave syrup

Method

Cover the oats with milk or water and cook over a gentle heat for 5 minutes or so until soft.

Serve with a generous helping of spices/nuts/seeds/berries and top with a drizzle of agave syrup.

Vital Tip:

If you normally add sugar to porridge, try a sprinkle of ground cinnamon instead; it will give a little natural sweetness and has been shown to help balance insulin and blood sugar levels.

Appley Pinhead Porridge

Pinhead porridge is a treat. It's a nuttier alternative to rolled oats, with a coarser texture. Just remember to soak overnight if you want it for breakfast tomorrow.

Ingredients

A handful of pinhead oats per person

½ cup of your choice of milk (e.g. semi-skimmed milk, or almond, hazelnut or coconut milk for a dairy-free version)

½ apple, coarsely grated

1-2 dsp sunflower seeds

Method

Soak the pinhead oats in water overnight in a small saucepan.

Next morning, add more water or your choice of milk and heat slowly over a gentle heat for 15-20 minutes until cooked (you can add more water or milk as you cook to achieve your desired consistency).

Stir in the grated apple and sunflower seeds to serve.

Muesli with a Twist

This muesli recipe is based on a traditional Bircher recipe. The key to its irresistible deliciousness is soaking all the ingredients overnight. Sounds weird, tastes fab!

Ingredients (about 4 servings)

4 handfuls of porridge oats

A handful each of mixed seeds – sunflower, pumpkin, sesame, linseed

2 handfuls of nuts, any you like (toasted hazelnuts are good!)

A handful of desiccated coconut (no added sugar – just check the label to be sure)

To serve:

1 apple, coarsely grated

Milk, or almond, hazelnut or coconut milk to cover

Natural yoghurt (leave this out if you prefer a dairy-free breakfast)

A handful of fresh berries – blueberries/raspberries/strawberries

Method

Combine the dry ingredients in an airtight container.

The night before you want to have this for breakfast, put a portion of the muesli mix into a bowl and add the grated apple. Cover with your milk of choice and leave overnight in the fridge.

Next morning, give it a stir to loosen the mixture before topping with natural yoghurt and some berries for a nutritious and delicious breakfast.

Vital Tip:

Make more and store! This recipe is perfect to make in bulk as it will store well in an airtight container.

Orange & Vanilla Granola

You are in for a treat with this granola! Breakfast cereals like granola can be expensive to buy and packed full of sugar, but it's so quick and easy to make from ingredients you probably already have in your larder. The combination of orange and vanilla in this recipe gives it a deliciously decadent flavour.

Ingredients (serves 6-8)

1 big juicy orange

2-3 tblsp agave syrup

½ vanilla pod

200g jumbo oats or spelt flakes (you can use rice flakes for a gluten-free version)

75g sunflower seeds

75g pumpkin seeds

50g flaked almonds

1 dsp mixed spice

1 tblsp rapeseed oil

Method

Preheat your oven to 160C/300F/Gas 2. Line a large baking tray with greaseproof or baking paper.

Put the zest and juice of the orange into a small saucepan with the agave syrup.

Remove the seeds from the vanilla pod by slicing it lengthways and scraping out the tiny black seeds with the point of a sharp knife. Add to the orange juice and heat very gently until simmering and the agave syrup has melted. Don't let the mixture boil.

Mix the dry ingredients in a bowl. Make a well in the middle and pour the orange juice mixture and rapeseed oil into it and mix well together.

Loosely spread the mixture onto the baking tray (or over 2 trays) and place into the oven for 25-30 minutes. Check it every 5-10 minutes to give it a shake and make sure the granola is colouring evenly.

Once it's ready, leave to cool and then store in an airtight container. This can be stored for up to a month (if it lasts that long!)

Eggy Breakfasts - three ways

Go to work on an egg for a perfectly healthy, low GL start to your day.

Eggs, glorious eggs!

1. **Boiled egg** with toasted pumpernickel rye bread soldiers and a little butter.

2. **Poached eggs** with wilted spinach, cherry tomatoes and red peppers – gently sauté the peppers and tomatoes in a non-stick pan. Add the spinach and cook until wilted. Poach the eggs. Serve the spinach mixture and eggs on toasted low GL bread (wholegrain or pumpernickel rye bread) or with steamed asparagus when it's in season.

3. **Scrambled eggs** with tomatoes and basil – allow about three eggs between two people. Whisk the eggs together, put into a medium non-stick pan and cook on a low heat. Chop a medium tomato and a handful of fresh basil and stir into your eggs. Add a little sea salt and some black pepper and serve with wholemeal toast or toasted pumpernickel rye bread.

Vital Tip:

If you prefer a carb-free option, just leave out the bread and have a few more vegetables on the side to keep your energy levels maintained and sustained.

Speedy Breakfast Ideas

If you are short of time and in need of a fast start to your day, kick-start your morning with one of these quick breakfasts.

Four 5-minute fixes:

1. Low sugar fruit (e.g. apple, pear, plum, kiwi, orange) with a handful of nuts and seeds – perfect to grab on the go and eat on the way to work if you are running late.

2. A high fibre, no-added-sugar breakfast cereal with 1-2 dsp milled seeds and milk of your choice.

3. Natural or Greek yoghurt with berries and seeds – add a drizzle of agave syrup if you like it a little sweeter.

4. Wholemeal bagel with cottage cheese (add sliced tomato and cucumber or smoked salmon for a luxurious treat).

Dave's Pomegranate & Red Grapefruit Salad

*I first tasted this on a fresh, crisp Swedish spring morning courtesy of my good friend Dave.
It is now a regular on my breakfast table.*

Ingredients (serves 2-4)

1 pomegranate
1 red grapefruit

Method

Scoop the pomegranate seeds into a bowl. An easy way to do this is by cutting the pomegranate in quarters and separating the seeds from the membrane with your fingers or a spoon.

With a sharp knife, segment the grapefruit, removing all the pith and place in the bowl with the pomegranate.

Vital Tip:

Serve as a weekend breakfast starter, or use as a topping on granola or muesli.

Quinoa Sunrise

Quinoa for breakfast may seem a little unusual, but it is a great, protein-based start to the day. I prefer using the grain, rather than quinoa flakes, which tend to have a very strong flavour.

Ingredients (serves 1)

2 tblsp cooked quinoa

A handful of mixed seeds (any mixture of sunflower, pumpkin, sesame, hemp or flaxseed)

Cinnamon, ground cloves, nutmeg or mixed spice

Low GL fruit of your choice (e.g. berries, sliced pear, grated apple)

A dollop of natural yoghurt

Method

Combine the quinoa and seeds in a breakfast bowl.

Sprinkle with your choice of spice and top with the fruit and yoghurt.

Vital Tip:

Quinoa Sunrise and Berry Nice Compote (page 154) make a great combination!

Healthy Eggy Bread

With just a few wee tweaks, eggy bread can make a healthy Sunday morning treat.

Ingredients (serves 2)

2-3 eggs

3 slices sourdough rye bread

Cinnamon

1 dsp agave syrup

Berries

Natural yoghurt

Method

Whisk the eggs in a flat bowl.

Place the bread in the egg mixture and soak well, coating both sides.

Heat a non-stick frying pan and lightly fry the soaked bread until golden on both sides.

Serve with a generous sprinkling of cinnamon, some fresh berries, a drizzle of agave syrup and a side of natural yoghurt.

Vital Tip:

Serve with cherry tomatoes and cottage cheese for a delicious savoury version.

Pumpernickel Rye Breakfast

Pumpernickel style rye bread is the bread of choice for a low GL diet. It makes a quick & filling breakfast if toasted and topped with a good protein source and will keep you feeling full for ages.

Here are a few ideas for toppers...

- Almond nut butter with a small banana, sliced.

- Cottage cheese, cherry tomatoes and fresh basil.

- Sugar-free peanut butter with smashed raspberries or strawberries.

- Low-fat cream cheese (or Quark), mixed with fresh dill, cucumber and a couple of slices of smoked salmon.

Think outside the lunchbox

Lunchtime recipes & ideas

Think outside the lunchbox...

No more soggy sandwiches or limp lettuce! It's time to give your lunchbox a makeover. Replace bread with pumpernickel rye, oatcakes, rye crispbread or wholemeal pitta pockets. Get creative with ingredients and try some of these suggestions for salads, pitta fillings or toppings for open sandwiches.

- **MONDAY** – Tuna & horseradish
  Tuna mixed with horseradish sauce, a dollop of natural yoghurt, black pepper, spring onions and chopped dill. Throw in some herby salad leaves, a sliced pepper and oatcakes for a Monday treat.

- **TUESDAY** – Go Greek
  Feta cheese, cucumber, peppers, olives, a few sunblush tomatoes, torn basil and a handful of salad leaves. Add some balsamic dressing and you have a tasty, Mediterranean-inspired lunch.

- **WEDNESDAY** – A Veggie Delight
  Sprouted beans, houmous and grated carrot stuffed into a wholemeal pitta pocket or served as an open sandwich on some pumpernickel rye bread.

- **THURSDAY** – Pesto Chicken
  Chicken, pesto, roasted red peppers, rocket, celery and a few sundried tomatoes make a tasty salad.

- **FRIDAY** – Eastern Promise
  Falafel, mixed salad leaves, raw vegetable crudités (carrot, celery, cucumber, peppers, sugar snap peas...) Great with a little houmous or tzatziki.

- **SATURDAY** – Halloumi and Chargrilled Vegetables
  Grilled halloumi cheese with leftover roasted Mediterranean vegetables (on page 116).

- **SUNDAY** – Omega Boost
  Smoked mackerel with sliced tomatoes, baby beets and green salad. Makes a brilliant Sunday brunch.

Five Spice Red Bean Soup

Adding beans and lentils to soups ensures you are ticking the protein box every time.

Ingredients (serves 6)

1 dsp coconut oil

1 onion, chopped

2 cloves garlic, crushed

1 celery stick, chopped

1 leek, chopped

1 carrot, chopped

1 tin adzuki or red kidney beans

1 tin chopped tomatoes

750ml vegetable stock

2 bay leaves

1 tsp Chinese Five Spice mix

3 cloves

Big handful of fresh coriander

Method

Put the oil in a large pan and heat. Add the onion and sweat for a couple of minutes until it starts to become translucent, then add the garlic, celery, leek and carrot and cook for a few minutes.

Drain and rinse the beans and add to the pan with the tomatoes, stock, bay leaves, Chinese Five Spice and cloves. Bring to the boil and allow to simmer for 10-15 minutes until the vegetables are tender.

Remove the bay leaf and the cloves before adding the chopped coriander and pulse in your blender or processor until the soup is blended but still has a bit of texture.

Spicy Tomato & Red Lentil Soup

Thanks to Nev for the inspiration for this budget cutting, nothing-in-the-cupboard soup recipe. Tinned tomatoes and a few lentils make this a filling and nourishing belly buster soup.

Ingredients (serves 4)

1 dsp coconut oil

1 onion, chopped

2 garlic cloves, crushed

3 sticks celery, chopped

2 bay leaves

1 red chilli, finely chopped

100g red lentils

1 tin chopped tomatoes

500ml vegetable stock

1 tblsp tomato puree

Sea salt & black pepper

Method

Heat the oil in a large, heavy based pan and cook the onion until translucent.

Add the garlic, celery, bay leaves and chilli and cook until the onions and celery have softened.

Add the lentils to the pan, with the tinned tomatoes, stock and tomato puree.

Bring to the boil, then reduce the heat and simmer gently until the lentils are cooked – about 20 minutes.

Season well.

Blitz in your blender until smooth.

Herby Mushroom & Puy Lentil Soup

This is an earthy, herby soup which tastes of autumn.

Ingredients (serves 4)

1 dsp coconut oil

1 onion, chopped

250g mushrooms, roughly chopped

2 garlic cloves, crushed

2 leeks, chopped

½ cup Puy lentils

2 bay leaves

A handful of fresh thyme

Generous handful of dried porcini mushrooms

1 litre chicken or mushroom stock

Generous handful of fresh parsley

Sea salt & black pepper

Method

Heat the oil in a heavy based saucepan.

Add the onion and cook until translucent. Add the mushrooms and cook for a few minutes until they start to colour.

Add the garlic and leeks and cook for a few minutes until the leek starts to soften.

Add the Puy lentils, bay leaf, thyme, dried mushrooms and stock. Bring to the boil and simmer for 15-20 minutes until the lentils are cooked.

Remove the bay leaves and stalks of the herbs. Add the fresh parsley, season well and pulse in your blender for a few seconds until roughly blitzed. It's best to leave this soup a little chunky, with the lentils intact.

Vital Tip:

Don't over-blitz this soup or you'll end up with grey sludge – guess how I know that?!

Thai Squash & Lentil Soup

The coconut milk and zesty lime make this soup a tasty treat. The lime juice adds a little acidic kick and has the added benefit of lowering the GL.

Ingredients (serves 6)

1 medium butternut squash

1 tsp coconut oil

1 onion, chopped

1-2 dsp Thai red curry paste

2 sticks celery

75g red lentils

750ml vegetable stock

1 tin coconut milk

1 inch root ginger, peeled and grated (about 1 tsp)

A handful of fresh coriander

1 lime – zest and juice

Method

Peel and quarter the butternut squash. Scoop out the seeds and cut into chunks.

Heat the oil in a large, heavy based pan with a lid and cook the onion until translucent.

Stir in the curry paste before adding the butternut squash, celery and lentils. Stir well to coat the vegetables and lentils. Add the stock, cover and simmer for 15-20 minutes until the lentils are tender and the squash has softened.

Take off the heat. Stir in the coconut milk, ginger, coriander and lime juice and zest.

Blitz in your blender until smooth and reheat if necessary.

Vital Tip:

This soup can be made with any root vegetable. Try carrot, parsnip or sweet potato when they are in season.

Speedy Pea & Mint Soup

Fast, green and delicious – what's not to love? Throw another pea in the pot!

Ingredients (serves 4)

1 dsp coconut oil
1 medium onion, chopped
500g frozen or fresh peas
750ml vegetable stock
A handful of fresh mint
Sea salt & black pepper

Method

Heat the coconut oil in a saucepan and add the onion. With the lid on the pan, allow to sweat until soft and translucent.

Place the peas in the pan with the stock, bring to a simmer and cook for five minutes, until the peas are tender.

Meanwhile, roughly chop the mint leaves.

Once the peas are cooked, add the mint leaves to the pan. Season well.

Blitz the soup with your blender.

carrot & Ginger Soup

This cookbook wouldn't be complete without a recipe from my lovely mum. This was one of our childhood favourites and really quite adventurous for the 1980s!

Ingredients (serves 4)

1 dsp coconut oil

1 large onion, chopped

6 medium carrots, chopped

75g red lentils

Pinch of dried chilli flakes

1 litre vegetable or chicken stock

1 inch root ginger, peeled and grated (about 1 tsp)

Juice and zest of ½ orange

Method

Heat the oil in a heavy based pan.

Add the onion and cook until translucent.

Add the carrots, lentils, chilli flakes and stock.

Simmer for 15 minutes, until the lentils are cooked.

Remove from the heat.

Grate in the root ginger and add the orange juice and zest.

Blitz in your blender until smooth.

Homemade Houmous

Houmous is packed full of essential nutrients like zinc, selenium and calcium as well as being a great source of healthy fats from olive oil and tahini. Ready-made houmous makes a really handy snack, but it's easy to make at home too.

Ingredients (serves 4)

1 tin chickpeas in water

2 tblsp (or more) lemon juice

2 or 3 garlic cloves, crushed

Generous pinch of sea salt

2 tblsp tahini

4 tblsp water

2 tblsp (or more) olive
or rapeseed oil

Method

Drain the chickpeas and rinse in a colander under the cold tap.

Place in your food processor with all the other ingredients except the oil.

Switch the processor on and pulse the ingredients together, drizzling the oil through the top of your food processor as you go. Stop when you have a creamy consistency.

Add more lemon juice, garlic or sea salt to taste.

Serve with oatcakes or as a dip with a selection of raw vegetables for a healthy snack.

Vital Tip:

Customise your houmous with a sprinkle of smoked paprika and a little dusting of cumin, or some freshly chopped parsley or coriander.

Pink Beetroot Houmous

Earthy, zingy and pink! This delicious houmous makes a vibrant change from the original recipe.

Ingredients (serves 4)

1 tin chickpeas

2 cooked beetroot

2 garlic cloves

Juice of 1 lemon

2 tblsp olive or rapeseed oil

Generous pinch of sea salt

½ tsp smoked paprika

Method

Drain and rinse the chickpeas, roughly chop the beetroot and then throw everything into your blender or food processor and blitz.

Simple as that!

Vital Tip:

Pink Beetroot Houmous will store in an airtight container in your fridge for a few days.

Herby Lime & Butter Bean Paté

Ingredients (serves 4)

1 tsp coconut oil

½ small onion, chopped

1 garlic clove, chopped

1 tin butter beans, drained and rinsed

Generous handful of fresh coriander and the same of parsley

Juice of 1 lime

1-2 tblsp olive oil or rapeseed oil

Sea salt & black pepper

Method

Gently heat the coconut oil in a small pan and soften the onion and garlic over a low heat.

Put this onion and garlic mix into your food processor with the butter beans, herbs and lime juice.

Switch the processor on and pulse the ingredients together, drizzling the olive or rapeseed oil in through the top of your food processor as you go. Stop when you have your desired consistency. Season well.

Serve on oatcakes or rye crispbread, or with vegetable sticks.

Smoked Mackerel Paté

This is a really simple recipe that is a taste sensation. Packed full of protein and essential fats, it's a nutritional hit too.

Ingredients (serves 4)

1 pack of smoked, peppered mackerel fillets

3-4 tblsp of cottage cheese

2 tsp horseradish sauce

½ lemon – zest and juice

Method

Remove the skin from the mackerel.

Place in a large bowl or your food processor, add the cottage cheese, horseradish sauce and lemon juice and zest.

Mash with a fork or blitz in your food processor until you have your preferred consistency.

Serve on oatcakes for a tasty snack or quick lunch.

Zesty Three colour Salad

Ingredients (serves 1-2)

100g feta cheese, cubed

1 large carrot, coarsely grated

2 sticks celery, finely chopped

A handful of fresh coriander, chopped

1 large orange, segmented

2 tblsp mixed seeds (any of sunflower, pumpkin, sesame, flax, hemp, poppy)

1 tblsp olive oil

Juice of 1 lemon

Black pepper

Method

Place the feta, carrot, celery, coriander and orange in a bowl.

Lightly toast the seeds in a large frying pan over a gentle heat until they are a golden brown colour.

Put the seeds into the bowl and add the olive oil and lemon juice.

Season well with black pepper.

Vital Tip:

This salad makes a delicious lunch, or for a more substantial meal serve with chicken or steamed fish.

Quinoa Super Salad

Quinoa used to be the mainstay of health food junkies, but is fast becoming a common ingredient in the regular lunchbox and on the menu of many local cafés and bistros. It's a seed, rather than a grain, making it a great protein source.

Ingredients
(serves 2 for a substantial lunch or 4 as a side salad)

250g ready cooked quinoa

A handful of sunflower and/or pumpkin seeds

3 or 4 spring onions, very finely chopped

Small carrot, grated

8 cherry tomatoes, halved

6-8 sunblush tomatoes, chopped

½ chilli, deseeded and finely chopped

½ red pepper, diced

1 avocado, peeled and cubed

100g feta cheese, cubed

A handful of fresh coriander, basil or flat leaf parsley, chopped

1 lemon – zest and juice

6 tblsp extra virgin olive oil or rapeseed oil

Sea salt & black pepper

Method

Place the ready cooked quinoa into a large bowl and separate out the grains with a fork.

Place the seeds in a dry frying pan and heat until golden. Be careful not to burn them. Add the seeds to the quinoa.

Add all prepared ingredients and mix gently. Season well.

Pack into a lunchbox and enjoy as a healthy alternative to sandwiches.

Tuscan Tuna & Bean Salad

Ingredients (serves 4)

1 tin red kidney beans or mixed beans

1 tin tuna, drained

1 avocado, diced

2 medium tomatoes, chopped

3 or 4 sunblush tomatoes, cut in half

1 celery stick, chopped

3 or 4 spring onions, chopped

½ red pepper, chopped

1 or 2 roasted red peppers, chopped

½ red chilli, finely chopped

Generous handful of parsley, chopped

Juice of 1 lemon

Olive or rapeseed oil

Sea salt & black pepper

Method

Drain and rinse the canned beans and put into a large bowl.

Add the tuna, avocado, tomatoes, sunblush tomatoes, celery, spring onions, red pepper, roasted peppers, chilli and parsley.

Squeeze the juice of the lemon over the salad and add a good glug of olive or rapeseed oil.

Season to taste.

Toss lightly to mix together.

Beet Slaw

What started out as a bit of an experiment has ended up as one of my favourite recipes. This makes a refreshing alternative to mayo-clad coleslaw, and is much better for you too.

Ingredients (serves 2-4)

1 or 2 big handfuls of sunflower and/or pumpkin seeds

1 or 2 raw beetroot, peeled and grated

1 carrot, peeled and grated

1 small red onion, finely sliced

Generous handful flat leaf parsley, chopped

1-2 tblsp apple cider vinegar

1-2 tblsp olive or rapeseed oil

Sea salt & black pepper

Method

Place the seeds in a dry frying pan and toast gently over a low heat for a few minutes until golden.

Combine in a bowl with the other ingredients and mix well.

Season to taste.

Vital Tip:

Try adding some grated apple for a zesty, fruity taste. This slaw is delicious served with some fresh grilled mackerel or the stuffed mushrooms on page 112.

Simple Salad Dressings

1. Classic French Dressing

2 tblsp olive oil

1 tblsp white wine vinegar
or cider vinegar

1 tsp Dijon mustard

Tiny pinch of sugar to taste

Salt & pepper

2. Honey & Mustard Dressing

2 tblsp olive oil or rapeseed oil

1 tblsp balsamic vinegar

1 tsp wholegrain mustard

½ tsp runny honey

Salt & pepper

3. Asian Dressing

Juice of 1 lime

1 tblsp rapeseed oil

½ tsp Chinese Five Spice

1 tsp soy sauce

1 tsp toasted sesame oil

1 tsp agave syrup

1 tsp Asian fish sauce

Method for all dressings

Place ingredients in a jar and shake until combined.
These salad dressings will keep fresh in your fridge for several days. Just remember to give them a shake before serving.

What's for dinner?

Dinner recipes

Satay stir-fry

Ingredients (serves 2)

For the sauce:

1 tblsp peanut butter
1 lime – zest and juice
2 garlic cloves, chopped
1 inch root ginger, grated
Dash of tamari or soy sauce
1 dsp nam pla (fish sauce) (optional)
1 tblsp natural yoghurt
1 red chilli, chopped
A handful of fresh coriander leaves

For the stir-fry:

1 tsp coconut oil
400g firm tofu or a large chicken breast
Wholemeal or buckwheat noodles
1 red, orange or green pepper, chopped
½ a head of broccoli cut into florets
1 carrot, sliced into strips
½ leek, sliced

Method

Blitz the sauce ingredients in your blender or food processor, adding a little water to thin the sauce to your preferred consistency. You can add more water at the cooking stage if necessary.

Put a little coconut oil in your wok and heat gently until melted.

Add the tofu or chicken to the wok and stir-fry until cooked, or the tofu is slightly golden.

Meanwhile cook your noodles according to the pack instructions.

Add the vegetables to your wok and keep on stir-frying. You want them nice and crunchy, so just a few minutes will do.

Add the sauce and stir-fry for another 2-3 minutes. Add more water at this stage if you need to.

Add the noodles to your wok and mix all the ingredients well.

Vital Tip:

Adding liquid to stir-fries reduces the cooking temperature and maintains the nutritional value of your grub.

Spicy Bean Hot Pot

Ingredients (serves 4-6)

1 tsp coconut oil

2-3 carrots, chopped

1 onion, chopped

1 large leek, chopped

1 parsnip, chopped

2-3 sticks celery, chopped

4 garlic cloves, crushed and roughly chopped

1 tblsp of tomato puree

1-2 chillies chopped (depending on how hot you like it)

1 tsp smoked paprika

1 jar passata or 2 tins chopped tomatoes

Glass of red wine or 250ml vegetable stock made with low salt stock cubes

2-3 bay leaves

2-3 tins of pulses – choose from adzuki, borlotti, butter, red kidney, chickpeas, etc.

Sea salt & black pepper

Method

Preheat your oven to 160C/300F/Gas 2.

Heat the oil in an ovenproof pan or casserole pot on the hob.

Add the carrots and onion and cook until the onion is soft and translucent.

Add the rest of the vegetables, garlic, tomato puree, chilli, paprika, tomatoes, red wine or stock, bay leaf and seasoning. Cook for 3-4 minutes. Add the beans.

Place the covered casserole dish into the oven for about an hour until the hotpot is bubbling, the vegetables are cooked and you are ready to eat.

Remove the bay leaf before serving.

Stuffed Portabello Mushrooms

Ingredients (serves 2)

4 Portabello mushrooms

¼ red pepper, chopped

¼ red onion, chopped

1 tomato, finely chopped

A handful of parsley, chopped

1 clove garlic, crushed and chopped

2-3 tsp Worcester sauce

1 small tub cottage cheese

Freshly ground black pepper

Method

Preheat the oven to 180C/350F/Gas 4.

Remove the stalks from the mushrooms and place on a flat ovenproof dish, open side up.

Mix the rest of the ingredients together in a bowl, season generously with black pepper and spoon into the centre of the mushrooms.

Bake for about 15 minutes until the mushrooms are soft.

Serve hot with a large fresh salad.

Vital Tip:

To make a vegetarian version, just replace the Worcester sauce with a little miso or soy sauce.

Vegetable Frittata

Ingredients (serves 2)

3 or 4 medium organic, free range eggs

1 tblsp cottage cheese

1 tsp coconut oil

½ red pepper, chopped

2 handfuls of frozen peas

½ leek, chopped

2 handfuls of spinach

7 or 8 sunblush tomatoes, chopped in half

A handful of fresh herbs, chopped (coriander, parsley or basil)

Sea salt & black pepper

Method

Whisk the eggs with the cottage cheese and season with freshly ground black pepper.

Heat the oil in a large omelette pan and add the pepper, peas and leek. Cook over a medium heat for a few minutes until slightly softened.

Add the spinach and sunblush tomatoes and cook for another minute or two until the spinach has wilted.

Pour on the egg mixture, add the herbs and cook over a medium heat until it starts to set.

Place under the grill on a medium heat for a further 10 minutes until set.

Serve with a green leafy salad.

Vital Tip:

This is a great way of using up leftover vegetables – an ideal Thursday night tea.

Herby Roasted Vegetables with Grilled Halloumi

Ingredients (serves 2)

½ aubergine

½ courgette

1 red onion

2 peppers (any colour)

A handful of cherry tomatoes

3 or 4 cloves of garlic

2 or 3 sprigs fresh rosemary or thyme

1 tblsp rapeseed oil

1 pack reduced fat halloumi cheese

Fresh basil

Sea salt & black pepper

Method

Preheat your oven to 180C/350F/Gas 4.

Chop the vegetables into bite-sized chunks and place onto a large roasting tray with the cherry tomatoes.

Keep the garlic in its skin, but crush with the flat side of a large knife.

Add the garlic and rosemary or thyme to the vegetables, drizzle with rapeseed oil and toss all the vegetables so they are evenly coated with oil.

Place in the preheated oven for about 45-50 minutes until the vegetables are cooked.

Heat a non-stick frying pan or griddle. Cut the halloumi into 6-8 slices and cook for about 2 minutes on each side until lightly browned. Remove from the heat and set aside until the vegetables are ready.

Serve the vegetables with the grilled halloumi and freshly torn basil.

Vital Tip:

Any leftover roasted vegetables will make a tasty lunch for tomorrow. Try them with a wholemeal pitta and some feta cheese.

Thai Fishcakes

Ingredients (serves 2)

150-200g white fish (choose sustainable fish like coley or pollock)

4 spring onions, chopped

1 inch fresh root ginger, grated

1 tsp Thai green curry paste

2 tsp nam pla (fish sauce)

1 egg, beaten

2 tblsp chopped coriander

1 tblsp flour (I use buckwheat flour, but whatever you have in the cupboard)

1 lime – zest and juice

Black pepper

1 tsp coconut oil

Method

Finely chop the fish and place in a large bowl with the spring onions, ginger, curry paste, fish sauce, egg and coriander. Mix well and then stir in the flour, lime juice and zest and season with black pepper.

The mixture may be a bit wet at this stage. You can add a bit more flour if you like.

Divide into 4 generous portions. Put a little flour on your hands and form each portion into a ball. Flatten slightly and fry in the coconut oil for 5-8 minutes until golden brown and cooked through.

Serve with a green salad or the Zingy Salsa on page 120.

Zingy Salsa with Crisp-skinned Mackerel

Ingredients (serves 2)

For the mackerel:

2 fresh mackerel, washed, scaled and gutted

Sea salt

1 lemon, sliced

For the salsa:

½ cucumber, finely chopped

½ red onion, finely chopped

2 medium tomatoes, chopped

1 red pepper, finely chopped

½ fresh chilli, finely chopped

2 tblsp fresh coriander, chopped

1 tblsp chives, chopped

Juice of 1 lime

1 tblsp olive oil

Freshly ground black pepper

Method

Preheat your grill to a high setting.

Using a sharp knife, score the skin of the mackerel diagonally three or four times on each side and season with salt. Put the sliced lemon in the cavity of the fish.

Place the mackerel onto a grill tray and grill for about 10 minutes and turn. Cook for another 10 minutes on this side until the fish is cooked through. Cooking time will vary depending on the size of your fish, so keep an eye on it.

For the salsa, place all the ingredients in a bowl and mix well together. Season to taste.

To serve, pile the salsa high on your plates alongside the mackerel.

Keralan Prawn Curry

Ingredients (serves 2)

500g tiger prawns, shells off & de-veined (fresh or frozen)

Juice of 1 lemon

1 tin coconut milk

Generous handful of fresh coriander

1 dsp coconut oil

1 onion, grated

2-3 garlic cloves, chopped

1 tsp root ginger, peeled and grated

½ tsp turmeric

6 cardamom pods, crushed

1 red chilli, finely chopped

1 cinnamon stick

1 red pepper, chopped

1 green pepper, chopped

½ head of broccoli, chopped into small florets

Sea salt

Method

Put the prawns in a non-metallic dish, add the lemon juice and allow to marinate.

Blitz the coconut milk and coriander in a blender or food processor.

Heat the coconut oil in a heavy based pan and add the onion and garlic. Cook until translucent.

Add the ginger, turmeric, cardamom, chilli and cinnamon stick. Cook for a further 2 minutes, stirring continuously.

Add the peppers and broccoli and cook for 2-3 minutes before adding the prawns and stir-frying until cooked.

Stir the coconut mix into the prawns and vegetables and gently simmer for 3-4 minutes.

Serve with brown basmati rice or quinoa.

Moroccan Chicken

Ingredients (serves 4)

1 tin chopped tomatoes

2 garlic cloves, crushed

1 tsp smoked paprika

1 tsp turmeric

½-1 tsp cayenne pepper

Big handful of flat leafed parsley

Pinch of sea salt & freshly ground black pepper

4 chicken breasts

1 red pepper, sliced

1 green pepper, sliced

1 pack (70g) pitted green olives

1 lemon, quartered

Method

Heat the oven to 180C/350F/Gas 4.

Combine the tomatoes, garlic, paprika, turmeric, cayenne and half of the parsley in your blender or processor and blitz to make a smooth sauce. Season with salt and pepper.

Place the chicken breasts in an ovenproof dish and score with a sharp knife about 4 times to let the sauce penetrate. Pour the sauce over the chicken. Add the peppers, olives and lemon slices.

Cover with foil and bake for 20 minutes, then remove the foil and cook for a further 10-15 minutes until the chicken is cooked through.

To serve, sprinkle with the remaining parsley and serve alongside some quinoa or brown rice and a fresh green salad.

Mediterranean chicken

Ingredients (serves 2)

2 chicken breasts

8 pitted black olives, halved

2-3 tsp capers

1 red onion, roughly chopped

6-8 cherry tomatoes

6-8 sunblush tomatoes

A handful of fresh basil

Freshly ground black pepper

Method

Preheat your oven to 180C/350F/Gas 4.

Place each of the chicken breasts on a sheet of foil, or in individual tinfoil dishes.

Keep half the basil aside for garnishing. Place all the other ingredients on top of the chicken and make a parcel with the foil, or place the lid onto the foil dishes. Season with black pepper.

Bake for about 25-35 minutes until the chicken is cooked through. Larger chicken breasts may take a little longer.

Sprinkle with freshly torn basil before serving with a large fresh salad.

Mini Spicy Bean Burgers

Ingredients (serves 4)

2 cans red kidney beans, drained
and rinsed

½-1 tsp chilli powder (depending on
how spicy you like it)

1 tsp ground cumin

1 tsp smoked paprika

1 tsp ground coriander

Small bunch flat leaf parsley,
chopped

1 lemon – zest and juice

1 medium, free range egg, beaten

Sea salt & black pepper

Coconut oil for frying

Method

Place the beans in a large bowl and mash with a fork or potato masher.

Stir in the spices, parsley, lemon juice, zest and beaten egg.

Season well.

Roll into about 6 or 8 small balls and flatten to make a burger shape.

Place in your freezer for about 30 minutes to chill before cooking.

Heat some coconut oil in a frying pan and gently fry until golden on either side.

Vital Tip:

These make a perfect mid-week dinner with the zingy salsa on page 120.

Salsa Verde with Pan Fried Salmon

Salsa Verde is a taste sensation and makes a perfect accompaniment for fish, chicken or steak.

Ingredients (serves 2)

For the salsa verde:

1 clove garlic, roughly chopped

Generous handful of parsley, basil and tarragon

2 tsp capers

1 tsp Dijon mustard

4 or 5 marinated anchovies

Juice of ½ lemon

2-3 tblsp olive or rapeseed oil

Black pepper

For the salmon:

2 wild salmon fillets

1 tsp coconut oil

Method

Place all the ingredients for the salsa verde in your blender and blitz to make a smooth sauce. You can add a little extra oil and/or lemon juice if it gets a bit sticky in your blender. Season to taste.

Heat the coconut oil in a large, non-stick frying pan over a medium heat. Cook the salmon, skin side down for 10-12 minutes until cooked through. Turn over and cook for another minute.

Vital Tip:

Serve alongside some seasonal steamed greens and keep any leftover salsa verde in an airtight container for a few days in the fridge.

Lamb Tagine

This stew is great to share with friends after a bracing autumn walk.

Ingredients (serves 4)

300g diced lamb

1 jar (about 90-100g) harissa paste

1 dsp coconut oil

1 onion, chopped

2 sticks celery, chopped

2 carrots, chopped

1 cinnamon stick

2 cloves garlic

1 tsp turmeric

70g pitted olives (green or black)

1 tin chickpeas

A handful of prunes, pitted dates or apricots

1 lemon

250ml beef or lamb stock

Generous handful flat leaf parsley

Method

Preheat the oven to 160C/300F/Gas 2.

Mix the harissa paste with the lamb and set aside while you prepare the rest of the tagine. If you have time, it is good to marinate the lamb in the harissa paste overnight in the fridge.

With a vegetable peeler, remove and save the rind of the lemon. Quarter the peeled lemon.

Heat the oil in a casserole dish on the hob.

Brown the marinated lamb and then add the onion, celery, carrot, cinnamon, garlic, turmeric, olives, chickpeas, dried fruit and lemon rind. Place the quartered lemon into the pot.

Add the stock, put the lid on the pot and transfer to the oven.

Cook for about 2 hours until the lamb is very tender.

Just before serving, top with parsley.

Delicious on its own or served with quinoa, brown rice or a crisp green salad.

Cauliflower Pizza

Anyone for pizza? This is a grain-free, low GL pizza with a difference.

Ingredients (serves 2)

For the crusts:

1 cauliflower, broken into florets

100g cream cheese

1 egg, beaten

Black pepper

For the tomato sauce:

1 tsp coconut oil

1 onion, finely chopped

3 garlic cloves, finely chopped

Pinch of dried chilli flakes

1 tin chopped tomatoes

A handful fresh basil, chopped

Sea salt & black pepper

Method

Preheat the oven to 200C/400F/Gas 6.

Line a baking tray with baking parchment.

Blitz the cauliflower in a food processor until powdery. Simmer in a pan of boiling water for 5 minutes. Drain and leave to cool before wrapping in a clean tea towel and squeezing to wring out excess water.

Place the cauliflower in a bowl and mix with the cream cheese and egg. Season well.

With clean hands, divide the mixture into four portions and shape on the lined baking tray to make a 1-1½ cm thick pizza base. Bake for 30-35 minutes, until firm and golden.

To make the sauce, heat the oil in a pan, add the onion and cook until translucent. Add the garlic, chilli and tomatoes and simmer for 10-15 minutes. Add fresh basil and blitz in your blender to make a smooth sauce.

Add a dollop of the tomato sauce and toppings of your choice to the cauliflower pizza base.

Bake for about 10 minutes.

Sara's Summer Curry

It is always a treat going to my friend Sara's house for dinner. She is a culinary whiz kid. In this recipe, she uses ginger for 'heat', rather than chilli, and uses summer veg, but you can use whatever vegetables are in season for a tasty supper at any time of the year.

Ingredients (serves 2)

4 chicken thighs

1-2 dsp coconut oil

1 onion, chopped

2 sticks of celery, chopped

2 garlic cloves, crushed and chopped

2 tsp ground cumin

2 tsp ground coriander

½ tsp turmeric

Pinch cayenne pepper

2 tblsp root ginger, finely grated

100g sugar snap peas (topped and tailed)

150g young spinach

1 tinned chopped tomatoes

250ml chicken stock

A handful of fresh coriander and mint

Juice of 1 lime

Sea salt & black pepper

Method

Heat the oil in a deep pan with a lid and add the chicken. Cook until coloured. Lift onto a plate and set aside.

Add the onion and celery to the pan with the remaining oil and cook slowly with the lid on until the onion is transparent. Add the garlic, ginger, coriander, cumin, turmeric and cayenne pepper and stir for 2-3 minutes.

Stir in the chicken, tomatoes, chicken stock and sugar snap peas. Bring to the boil and allow to simmer for 20 minutes stirring occasionally.

Finally add the chopped spinach, season to taste and cook for a further two minutes before serving with the freshly chopped coriander, mint and squeeze of lime.

Quick Quinoa Kedgeree

Try saying that in a hurry! Kedgeree is traditionally a breakfast dish, but it makes a great mid-week dinner and if there are any leftovers you can pack it into a lunchbox too.

Ingredients (serves 4)

1 cup quinoa

2 spring onions, finely chopped

1 clove garlic, finely chopped

3 tsp garam masala

1 tsp turmeric

3 bay leaves

1 stick celery, chopped

1 tsp root ginger, grated

150g frozen peas

1 packet smoked, peppered mackerel, skinned and roughly flaked

2-4 eggs, hard boiled

1 large bunch flat leaf parsley, roughly chopped

Method

To cook the quinoa, place in a saucepan with two cups of water. Bring to the boil and simmer for 10 minutes with the lid on. Take off the heat and leave to stand for a further 10 minutes until all the water has soaked up.

Add the spring onions, garlic, garam masala, turmeric and bay leaves to the quinoa and heat gently.

Add the celery and ginger to the quinoa mixture and cook for 1-2 minutes. Then add the peas and cook for another 1-2 minutes.

Stir in the flaked mackerel and parsley.

To serve, remove the bay leaf before quartering the hard boiled eggs and placing on top.

Asian Beef Salad

This salad makes a filling high protein, low GL meal.

Ingredients (serves 2 or 3)

1-2 tblsp oyster sauce

1 clove garlic, chopped

½ to 1 chilli (depending on how hot you like it), chopped

200g fillet steak, thinly sliced

1 tsp coconut oil

For the salad:

3 or 4 spring onions, chopped

100g beansprouts

1 red pepper, sliced

¼ cucumber

Bunch of coriander, chopped

A few strips of preserved ginger

2 tblsp sesame seeds

Method

Mix the oyster sauce, garlic and chilli together in a bowl and add the sliced steak. Allow to marinate while you make the salad.

In a salad bowl, combine the spring onions, beansprouts and red pepper. Use a vegetable peeler to finely slice the cucumber into strips. Add to the other salad ingredients. Add the chopped coriander and preserved ginger.

Put the sesame seeds into a heavy based pan and heat gently until lightly toasted. Add to the salad.

Heat the coconut oil in a wok, then add the marinated beef and stir-fry for a couple of minutes until cooked.

Serve the beef along with the salad and add dressing to taste.

Vital Tip:

Add the Asian Salad Dressing on page 104 for a little extra flavour if you fancy it.

chicken & Fennel Bake

Ingredients (serves 2)

1 fennel bulb, sliced

1 red pepper, sliced

12 cherry tomatoes

2 cloves garlic (keep the skin on)

2 chicken breasts or 4 thighs

Generous drizzle of rapeseed oil

Sea salt & black pepper

Method

Preheat your oven to 180C/350F/Gas 4.

Layer the fennel, pepper and tomatoes in an ovenproof dish with a lid.

Add the garlic cloves and place the chicken on top. Season well.

Drizzle over a little rapeseed oil and roast for about 25-30 minutes until the chicken is cooked through.

Serve with a green salad and a dollop of Salsa Verde (page 130) on the side.

sweet treats

Dessert recipes

Lightly Spiced Poached Pears

Pears are low GL, packed full of fibre and grow locally. What's not to love, especially when they can taste this good?

Ingredients (serves 4)

4 pears

300ml apple juice

Juice of 1 lemon

2 cinnamon sticks

4 cloves

1 dsp agave syrup

To serve:
70% cocoa chocolate

Method

Peel the pears, leaving the stalks intact. Cut the bottom off the pears so they will sit flat on a plate for serving.

Place in a saucepan with the apple juice, lemon juice and enough water to cover. Add the cinnamon stick, cloves and agave syrup.

Place on a medium heat and gently bring to the boil. Simmer for 15-20 minutes and take off the heat. Leave to infuse in the syrup for an hour or so until cooled.

Serve on a puddle of melted dark chocolate.

Plum & Ginger Crumble

Usually packed full of fat and sugar, crumble may not spring to mind as a healthy dessert, but here's a nutritious twist on an old favourite.

Ingredients (serves 3 or 4)

6 or 8 plums (depending on size)
6 pieces of crystallised ginger, chopped
1 tblsp maple syrup

For the crumble:
50g butter or coconut oil
75g wholemeal spelt flour
50g porridge oats

Vital Tip:

Make multiple amounts of the crumble topping and store in portion sizes in your freezer. Use as required on top of any stewed fruit when you fancy a treat.

Method

Preheat your oven to 200C/400F/Gas 6.

With a sharp knife, halve the plums and place in a saucepan with the crystallised ginger, maple syrup and one tablespoonful of water. Leave the stones in the plums as they are easier to remove after cooking. Simmer over a gentle heat until the plums are soft.

Meanwhile, make the crumble topping by rubbing the butter into the flour and oats in a large bowl until fully mixed and crumbly.

When the plums are cooked, allow to cool a little before removing the stones and placing in an ovenproof dish.

Spread the crumble mixture on top and bake for about 20 minutes, until golden and bubbling.

Serve with Greek yoghurt or good quality vanilla ice cream for a wee touch of decadence.

Cinnamon Nectarines with Vanilla Scented Yoghurt

Ingredients (serves 2)

1-2 tsp agave syrup

2 nectarines, halved with stone removed

½-1 tsp ground cinnamon

½ vanilla pod

2 tblsp Greek yoghurt

Method

Preheat your oven to 180C/350F/Gas 4.

Drizzle a little agave syrup over each nectarine half and sprinkle with cinnamon. Cover with tinfoil and bake for 15-20 minutes until soft.

Slice the vanilla pod lengthways and, with the tip of a sharp knife, scrape out the seeds and stir into the Greek yoghurt.

Serve the nectarines hot or cold with a drizzle of agave syrup and a dollop of the vanilla scented Greek yoghurt.

Cardamom & Orange Choc Pots

Who can resist a chocolate mousse, especially if there is any chance that the contents might actually be good for you? This is a dairy-free mousse that tastes wickedly divine.

Ingredients

6 cardamom pods

100ml almond milk

2 eggs

100g 70% cocoa chocolate

Zest of half an orange

A handful of hazelnuts

Method

Crush the cardamom pods and put into a small pan with the almond milk. Bring to the boil over a gentle heat.

Separate the egg whites from the yolks, but keep both parts.

Melt the chocolate by breaking it into squares and placing it in a bowl over a pan of hot water. Keep stirring until completely melted.

Strain the milk through a tea strainer or muslin cloth to remove the cardamom pods.

Whisk the yolks until thick, then add slowly to the melted chocolate with half the orange zest and the strained milk.

Whisk the egg white until it forms soft peaks and then fold the egg white into the chocolate mixture until fully mixed.

Pour into ramekins or espresso cups.

Leave to cool then cover with clingfilm and refrigerate for a few hours.

Decorate with the remaining orange zest and serve with a few hazelnuts.

Berry Nice compote

Quick and simple to make, this delicious compote makes a tasty dessert with a dollop of Greek yoghurt or good quality ice cream.

Ingredients

1 bag frozen berries

1 star anise

1 cinnamon stick

3 cardamom pods

1-2 dsp agave syrup

Method

Place all the ingredients in a saucepan and heat gently until the berries have defrosted and a syrup starts to form (about 5-10 minutes). Don't overcook as you will end up with mushy berries.

Before serving, remove the star anise, cinnamon stick and cardamom pods.

Vital Tip:

Berry Nice Compote will keep in the fridge for several days. It makes a delicious addition to porridge or Quinoa Sunrise on page 66 for breakfast too.

Snack attack

Snack recipes

Super Snacks

Remember the old days when snacks were seen as dietary 'sins' and the idea of healthy eating was starving yourself until you felt weak, dizzy and irritable?! Thankfully, those days are (mostly) gone. Most nutrition experts now agree that eating little and often is far preferable.

As long as you make the right choices for healthy snacks, eating small amounts more frequently can help boost your energy levels, balance your weight and banish sugar cravings. Grazing regularly on the right stuff means you won't feel hungry, making it easier to resist chocolate bars, crisps and sugary snacks that sap your energy levels and leave you wanting more.

Most supermarkets carry a good range of healthy snacks, ideal for eating on the run or if you have forgotten to pack a snack for the day. Wasabi peas, soya nuts and toasted beans can be found in the healthy eating aisle, alongside little packs of chilli or herb flavoured nuts and seeds. These can make a tasty alternative to the plain versions every now and again. There are even a few companies producing oat baked snacks, which make a great substitute for crisps. Have a look around your local health food shop to see what you can find.

Snack packs of olives can make a quick and tasty nibble too and plenty of supermarkets, delis and cafés produce houmous in bite-sized portions with a few carrot sticks.

If you are caught on the hop and are relying on your local corner shop for a quick snack, grab a pot of natural or Greek yoghurt from the fridge. If you are super-hungry, have it with a banana (not too ripe though, as the riper the banana is, the more concentrated its sugar content). Even in the most basic shop, it should be possible to pick up something healthy to keep you going.

Naturally, we think of fruit as a perfect snack food – served up ready to eat from Mother Nature, packed full of essential vitamins, minerals, fibre and trace elements. To help sustain your energy levels, it's best to choose lower sugar fruit and combine it with a little protein – just a few nuts or seeds will do the trick.

Luckily, eating lower sugar fruit also means choosing local varieties, because fruit that is grown in temperate climates (like the UK and Ireland) tends to have a lower sugar load than tropical fruit. This also has the added benefit that your fruit will have travelled fewer food miles and so will be packed with more nutrients than if it had to travel halfway around the world to make it into your fruit bowl.

Keep fruit intake to a maximum of 3 portions a day, and eat it, don't drink it. Although fruit juice has a healthy reputation, it's a sure-fire way to bump up your sugar intake. One glass of orange juice can contain 3 or 4 oranges. That's a big sugar hit! Some juices and smoothies contain as much sugar as a can of fizzy pop. It's much better to make your own smoothies, keeping the fruit content low and adding a little protein for sustained energy release.

Choose these:

- **Apples**
- **Pears**
- **Plums**
- **Berries (strawberries, blueberries, blackberries, raspberries)**
- **Cherries**
- **Grapefruit**
- **Oranges**
- **Kiwis**
- **Nectarines**
- **Peaches**
- **Fresh apricots**
- **Avocado**
- **Cantaloupe or honeydew melon**
- **Lemons**
- **Mandarins**
- **Fresh watermelon**

Instead of these:

- **Dried fruit**
- **Tropical fruit like pineapple or mango**
- **Fruit juices**
- **Dates**

Easy, Portable Snacks

Here are some tried and tested ideas for healthy snacks on the run.

- A selection of unroasted, unsalted nuts and/or seeds in a small plastic pot with a sealed lid. Choose from almonds, hazelnuts, brazils, cashews, pecans or walnuts, sunflower or pumpkin seeds.

- Two oatcakes with nut butter. Look out for sugar-free peanut butter – most supermarkets now stock it. If you are not a fan of peanut butter, there are plenty of other alternatives, including cashew, almond or hazelnut butter. Oatcakes and nut butter make a tasty, low sugar alternative to biscuits.

- Houmous with carrot sticks, red pepper or celery.

- Nutty apple slices – just chop up an apple and spread a little sugar-free peanut butter on top for a quick and tasty treat at any time of the day.

- A handful of cherry tomatoes.

- A small avocado.

- Low sugar oat biscuits – some brands produce handy sized snack packs, ideal for a quick snack and great as an occasional treat. Some of them come ready packaged as two biscuits so you will be less likely to go overboard.

- Need a chocolate hit? How about a couple of squares of really dark chocolate (at least 70% cocoa content) with 3 or 4 brazil nuts.

- A piece of fruit (maybe an apple, a pear, a couple of plums or a kiwi) with 5-6 almonds (or any low sugar fruit, combined with any nut – as long as it's not salted or roasted).

- Natural yoghurt with fresh berries (blueberries, raspberries, strawberries) in a sealable pot. Add a squirt of agave syrup if you prefer a sweeter tasting yoghurt. Try out a few different brands of yoghurt to see which you like best – some taste sharper and others are creamier. It's your choice.

Cranberry & Coconut Flapjacks

This recipe uses dried fruit and low GL maple syrup instead of sugar.

Ingredients (makes about 25 bite-size pieces)

125g cranberries

175g chopped dates

200ml water

60g coconut oil

60g butter

3 tblsp maple syrup

250g porridge oats

2 tblsp desiccated coconut

3 tblsp seeds – sunflower, pumpkin and linseeds

You will need: a cake tin or baking tray approx 18cm x 18cm – lined with baking parchment or greaseproof paper.

Method

Preheat your oven to 180C/350F/Gas 4.

Place the cranberries and dates in a small saucepan with the water and bring to the boil. Simmer gently until the fruit has softened and the water has soaked into the fruit, adding a little more water if you need to.

In another pan, melt the coconut oil, butter and maple syrup together over a low heat.

Mix the oats, coconut and seeds together in a large bowl, make a well in the middle and pour in the melted syrup and butter mixture.

Stir in the softened dried fruit and mix well.

Tip the mixture onto a lined baking tray, spread it out evenly and press down firmly with the back of a metal spoon or palette knife.

Bake for about 25-35 minutes until golden brown.

Allow to cool for 10 minutes before cutting into squares.

Once cooled, store in an airtight container.

Chocolate Orange Boost Balls

The perfect thing if you are in need of a chocolate hit without the sugar overload. These little gems taste like just the kind of thing you shouldn't be allowed to eat on a low GL diet.

Ingredients

4 tblsp peanut butter (smooth or crunchy? It's your call)

2 tblsp agave syrup

2 tblsp cocoa powder, plus extra for coating

Zest of one orange

1 tblsp freshly squeezed orange juice

Method

Put all the ingredients into a mixing bowl and mix together with a fork.

Make into about 12-15 balls using your hands.

Roll in cocoa powder and enjoy (without feeling guilty!)

Mega Cinnamonny Apricot Flapjacks

Ingredients (makes about 24)

200g porridge oats

2 tblsp desiccated coconut

3 tblsp seeds (sunflower, pumpkin and linseeds)

2 tblsp ground cinnamon

150g unsulphured dried apricots, finely chopped

150ml water

100g coconut oil (or butter)

4 tblsp agave syrup

You will need: a cake tin or baking tray approx 18cm x 18cm – lined with baking parchment or greaseproof paper.

Method

Preheat the oven to 180C/350F/Gas 4.

Measure the porridge oats, coconut, seeds and cinnamon into a mixing bowl.

Place the chopped apricots in a small saucepan with the water and simmer gently, stirring until all the water has soaked up and the apricots are sticky. Add the apricots to the dry ingredients.

Melt the coconut oil and agave syrup together in a small saucepan over a gentle heat. Add to the other ingredients and mix well together.

Tip the mixture into a greased or lined swiss roll tin, pressing down firmly using the back of a metal spoon.

Bake for about 25-35 minutes until golden.

Allow to cool for 10 minutes before cutting into squares.

Once cooled, store in an airtight container.

Rosemary Crackers

These crackers are fast, easy to make and taste totally delicious. If you are seeking a grain-free alternative to crackers and oatcakes, then give them a go.

Ingredients

100g sunflower seeds

100g ground almonds

2 tblsp fresh rosemary, chopped

Generous pinch of sea salt

1 tblsp rosemary & garlic infused rapeseed oil (or just plain rapeseed or olive oil if you don't have this)

1 egg

Method

Preheat your oven to 180C/350F/Gas 4.

Put the sunflower seeds into your food processor and blitz to a powdery consistency. Add the ground almonds and chopped herbs and pulse until mixed, then put the mixture into a bowl.

Whisk the egg with the rapeseed oil and fold this into the dry ingredients. Turn out onto a sheet of baking parchment paper, place another layer of paper on top and roll the mixture between the two sheets until it is about ½ cm thick. Remove the top layer of paper. Gently lift the bottom layer with the mixture on it and slide onto a baking tray.

Score with a sharp knife into bite size squares.

Bake for about 25-30 minutes until golden.

Leave to cool, store in an airtight container and serve with houmous or cottage cheese.

Paleo Banana Bread

This is a grain-free, dairy-free, protein-rich banana bread for a sustained energy kick that keeps on giving.

Ingredients

1 tblsp coconut oil

120g ground almonds

1 tsp baking soda

¼ tsp sea salt

1 dsp cinnamon

3 eggs

3 bananas, not too ripe

2 tblsp dessicated coconut

30g crystallised ginger, chopped

You will need: a 1lb loaf tin

Method

Preheat your oven to 180C/350F/Gas 4 and line a loaf tin with baking parchment or greasproof paper.

Melt the coconut oil in a small saucepan and place the almonds, baking soda, salt and cinnamon in your blender or food processor and mix well. Add the eggs, one at a time and then pour in the melted coconut oil. Pulse in your processor until fully mixed.

Chop in the bananas, add the desiccated coconut and crystallised ginger. Pulse gently until mixed.

Pour the batter into the prepared loaf tin.

Bake for 30-40 minutes. To check it's ready, a skewer inserted into the middle of the loaf should come out clean.

Allow to cool slightly in the loaf tin and then transfer onto a wire rack to cool.

Seven day plan

Ready to get started? This 7 day plan will get you off to a flying start. Don't feel you have to stick to it rigidly, it's just to give you some ideas.

Follow these simple guidelines to help keep you on track:

- Drink up. Aim for around 1½ litres water a day. Start your day with a cleansing mug of hot water and a slice of lemon. Herbal teas will count towards your water intake, but tea and coffee don't. If you are not too keen on the taste of water, add a couple of wedges of orange or a few slices of lime to give it a wee bit of flavour.

- Eat oily fish 3 times a week. Choose from salmon, mackerel, herring, trout or sardines. Fresh, tinned or frozen all count towards your weekly intake.

- Have some green leafy vegetables every day. A big salad at lunchtime, some steamed greens with dinner or add some greens to soups and stews to get your daily quota.

- Eat more vegetables than fruit. Try raw carrots, peppers, celery or sugar snap peas for a quick snack with some houmous as an alternative to fruit, but aim high – at least seven portions of fruit and vegetables every day.

- Invest in a food flask so you can take leftover dinner into work for lunch the next day.

- Eat some nuts and seeds every day. Have a handful with a piece of fruit as a snack, some nut butter on oatcakes for a mid-afternoon treat or add ground seeds to porridge, granola or yoghurt.

- If you are out and about, carry some nuts and seeds in a container with you for a quick and easy snack.

- Eat some new foods. The more variety you have in your diet, the better. When you are shopping for fruit and vegetables, why not pick up something you have never tasted before, or buy a vegetable that you haven't had for ages? It could be something as simple as choosing cauliflower instead of broccoli this week, or bringing home a sweet potato to bake instead of mashed spuds every night. Variety will do your health the world of good.

	Breakfast	Snack	Lunch	Snack	Dinner
Day 1	Orange and Vanilla Granola (page 58)	Apple and a handful of almonds	Herby Mushroom & Puy Lentil Soup (page 80) with Rosemary Crackers (page 168) and cottage cheese	Cranberry & Coconut Flapjack (page 162)	Satay Stir-fry (page 108) with buckwheat soba noodles
Day 2	Poached eggs with toasted pumpernickel rye bread (page 60)	2 oatcakes with houmous (page 88)	Smoked Mackerel Paté (page 94) with raw vegetable crudités and rye crispbread	Chopped apple topped with sugar-free peanut butter	Mini Spicy Bean Burgers (page 128) (don't forget to save some for tomorrow's lunch) with Beet Slaw (page 102)
Day 3	Quinoa Sunrise (page 66)	Pear and a handful of walnuts	Leftover Mini Spicy Bean Burgers from last night, with a green salad	Berries with natural yoghurt	Sara's Summer Curry (page 136) with brown basmati rice or quinoa
Day 4	Scrambled eggs with tomatoes and basil on toasted pumpernickel rye (page 60)	A slice of Paleo Banana Bread (page 170)	Quinoa Super Salad (page 98)	Small pot of natural yoghurt with Berry Nice Compote (page 154)	Thai Fishcakes (page 118) with Zingy Salsa (page 120)
Day 5	Muesli with a Twist (page 56)	Kiwi with a handful of sunflower seeds	Tuscan Tuna & Bean Salad (page 100)	2 oatcakes with almond or sugar-free peanut butter	Stuffed Portabello Mushrooms (page 112) with a great big, colourful fresh salad
Day 6	Healthy Eggy Bread with fresh berries and natural yoghurt (page 68)	Carrot & celery sticks with Pink Beetroot Houmous (page 90)	Beet Slaw (page 102) with tinned mackerel	Herby Lime & Butter Bean Paté (page 92) with carrot sticks	Asian Beef Salad (page 140)
Day 7	Perfect Porridge (page 52)	Pear and a handful of hazelnuts	Thai Squash & Lentil Soup (page 82) with oatcakes	Chocolate Orange Boost Balls (page 164)	Cauliflower Pizza (page 134) with green salad

Your checklist for energy and vitality

1. Eat real food – no processed junk, just good quality, fresh foods, and plenty of variety.

2. Break your fast – eat within 45 minutes of getting up.

3. Get grazing – eat little and often, every 3 or 4 hours.

4. Power yourself with protein – munch on a little bit of protein with every meal and snack.

5. Quit the energy zappers – sugar, stimulants and refined carbs are the biggies, so cut them back.

6. Get down with the GL – choose slow release carbs that are packed with fibre to keep you sustained and maintained.

7. Buy local – support your community's food heroes and buy local produce in season.

8. Shop regularly – you'll have fresher, more nutritious grub and less food waste.

9. Take healthy short cuts – check out the frozen food aisles for herbs, quality frozen veg, fruit and fish.

10. Make in bulk – cook more than you need for an extra portion to freeze or for tomorrow's lunch. Much healthier (and cheaper) than soggy sandwiches and a packet of crisps.

11. Stock a healthy store cupboard – pack your larder with some key ingredients such as eggs, tinned tomatoes, coconut milk, pulses, herbs and spices so you can throw together a quick and healthy meal any night of the week.

12. Remember the 80:20 rule – a little of what you fancy does you good. Healthy eating should never be taken to extreme measures. Everything in moderation!

Your food diary

Keeping a food diary can help you to focus on making a few positive changes to your diet.
Record everything you eat and drink for one week to see where you could make some adjustments.

	Breakfast	Snack	Lunch	Snack	Dinner
Monday					
Tuesday					
Wednesday					
Thursday					
Friday					
Saturday					
Sunday					

Eat your way to
energy and vitality!